WINDOWS
ON·THE·WORLD

·HOW·
PEOPLE
·LIVED·

Written by
Dr Anne Millard

Illustrated by
Sergio

Macmillan of Canada
A Division of Canada Publishing Corporation
Toronto, Ontario, Canada

Editor Jane Elliot
Series Art Editor Roger Priddy
Series Editor Angela Wilkes

Managing Editor Vicky Davenport

First published in Canada in 1989
by Macmillan of Canada
A Division of Canada Publishing Corporation,
Toronto, Ontario, Canada

First published in Great Britain in 1989
by Dorling Kindersley Limited
9 Henrietta Street, London WC2E 8PS

Copyright © 1989
Dorling Kindersley Limited, London

Canadian Cataloguing in Publication Data

Millard, Anne
  How people lived.

(Windows on the world)
Includes index.
ISBN 0-7715-9642-1

1. Civilization, Ancient – Juvenile literature.
2. Civilization, Medieval – Juvenile literature.
I. Sergio.   II. Title.

CB311.M54 1989   930   C88-094830-2

Phototypeset by Southern Positives and Negatives (SPAN)
Reproduced in Singapore by Colourscan
Printed in Spain by Artes Graficas, Toledo S.A.
D. L. TO:2005 -1988

CONTENTS

PEOPLE FROM THE PAST

Over the years people's basic needs have changed little. In this book you can join your ancestors from thousands of years ago emerging from their caves wearing animal skins. Or you can go back hundreds of years and see a banker in his house dressed in rich clothes and furs. Both the caveman and the banker have things in common with each other and with us because we all have similar needs, such as food, drink and shelter.

Although people have always needed protection from the burning sun or the bitter cold, over the years their shelter and clothing have changed. People soon learnt that their food tasted better if it was cooked over fire, and that they could grow food for their families and animals.

Through the pages of this book you will see how your ancestors lived, discover their likes and fears and explore their houses, which have been specially drawn to let you see inside.

Meet the people
Here are some of the people you will meet in this book. Some are extremely tough because of the harsh conditions in which they live, others live in the lap of luxury.

Ban and Uro
You will begin your journey in what is now France, in around 13,000 B.C. when Europe is in the grip of an Ice Age. Find out how Ban and his father Uro survive by hunting for meat with flint spears.

Illa
Illa lives in what is now Iran at a time when a vitally important change in human history is taking place. It is around 10,000 B.C., and as she gathers in the harvest, Illa is part of a new way of life: farming.

Kai and his mother
Kai belongs to a Celtic tribe living in central Europe in about 500 B.C.. His family are metal smiths and he is learning from them. His mother spends hours cooking in their large hut.

Rudek
Rudek is a chief living in about 500 B.C. in Siberia, near the Altai Mountains. He joins his men herding their horses to new pastures. Life in the saddle is especially hard during the freezing winters.

Lysander and Thea
Around 424 B.C. the city of Athens in Greece is producing some of the greatest thinkers, writers and artists known. Thea and Lysander live with their parents, and are considerate to their slaves.

Lady Ch'eng
In around 130 B.C. the Han emperor's consort lives quietly in her palace, surrounded by beautiful gardens. But Lady Ch'eng gives her son a terrible shock when she goes to inspect his new horse.

Rasfa
The new prosperity brought about by farming, means that towns grow and people have new needs. In about 6000 B.C. the people of Çatal Hüyük in Turkey start trading. Rasfa is always the first to make a deal.

Ashnan
In Mesopotamia in about 2050 B.C., it is pleasant to live in an organized city where rulers and priests protect and care for you. But there is always a price to pay and Ashnan's family have to sell her.

Hori
Hori lives in Egypt in about 1480 B.C. when the Egyptian civilization is at the height of its greatness. Watch Hori's family take part in a ceremony, and learn how a brother becomes a mummy.

Princess Dictynna
Meet Dictynna, a princess on the Mediterranean island of Crete in about 1480 B.C.. She lives a life of great comfort in a brightly painted palace. Like the rest of the Cretans, she loves the sea.

Claudius and Livia
Senator Claudius and his family live in a lavish house in the imperial city of Rome in about 20 B.C.. While every free man is a citizen like Claudius, you will see that not everyone lives in such luxury.

Eric
You can find the Viking blacksmith Eric working in a village in Norway in about A.D. 950. He is a skilled craftsman and his fine swords are valued by his violent friends who plunder distant shores.

Brother William
You might find that life in an English village in around A.D. 1320 seems more familiar, but if you kept the same hours as Brother William you would realize how different it is for a medieval monk.

Francesco
In the Renaissance town of San Vitale in A.D. 1450, you will discover how Francesco spends the money he has made in his bank. He is usually patronizing a new poet or artist, or entertaining.

IN THE SHELTER OF THE CAVE

You have travelled back in time to the year 13,000 B.C. and find yourself in the Stone Age. You are in a wooded river valley in what is now southwest France. The climate is much colder than nowadays, as Europe is in the final stages of an Ice Age, and France is rather like northern Russia or Canada are today. It is late summer and a group of people are setting up camp in the mouth of a cave.

We are directly descended from people like those shown here. The scientific name for them is *homo sapiens*, which means "thinking man", but they are often called Cro-Magnon Man, after the cave in France where their remains were first discovered. Like people who lived before them, the Cro-Magnons lived by hunting, fishing and gathering wild plants to eat. They spent their lives moving from place to place in search of food, living in tents or sheltering in caves. The Cro-Magnons were not just hunters; besides their great knowledge of animals and plants, they left behind many tools, weapons and paintings which show that they were skilled craftsmen and talented artists.

Setting up camp
Here and on the next two pages you can see the tribe setting up camp outside one of the many limestone caves in the area. Ban belongs to this tribe and he and his father Uro have been hunting.

Instant housing
Ban's tribe lives in tents in the open for part of the year, but when the winter snows come the tribe moves the tents into the caves, perhaps building a windbreak of stones across the entrance.

Telling tales
Life is hard and many people die young. Old people are valued members of the tribe as they pass on their skills and wisdom to the children. This old man is describing a great hunt.

A blazing fire
A fire has been started in preparation for cooking. This tribe starts a fire by striking a lump of *pyrite*, a special kind of rock, with a flint. This is much quicker than rubbing two wooden sticks together.

Tent building
Nomads are people who move around the land and set up camp in areas that produce better hunting and fishing. Ban's tribe is nomadic, and after arriving at their location, they make their tents from animal hides thrown over frameworks of wooden poles and weighted down with heavy stones.

Thick-skinned
The Cro-Magnons wear warm clothes made of animal hides and fur. They have invented a needle made of bone, so they can sew the animal skins together. They often decorate their clothes with beads, teeth and shells.

On a knife's edge
The tribe are skilled toolmakers. They use flint to make sharp, efficient blades for their knives, spears, axes, scrapers and chisel-like tools called *burins*. They also make tools from antlers, bones and ivory. Archaeologists today can tell one group of cave-dwelling hunters of the past from another by their tools.

7

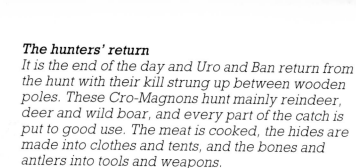

The hunters' return

It is the end of the day and Uro and Ban return from the hunt with their kill strung up between wooden poles. These Cro-Magnons hunt mainly reindeer, deer and wild boar, and every part of the catch is put to good use. The meat is cooked, the hides are made into clothes and tents, and the bones and antlers into tools and weapons.

Food for the future

While the men go hunting, some of the women gather plants, roots and berries in leather bags and rush baskets. They will store these for the winter, when food is scarce.

Spears and harpoons

The Cro-Magnons hunt in groups, if they are following large animals, and have invented tools to increase their chances of success. These include spear-throwers, which enable them to hurl their spears further and with greater force, and harpoons that the animals cannot shake free.

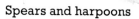

How do we know?

We know how important animals were to the Cro-Magnons from the magnificent rock paintings found deep within some of their caves. The pictures are mostly of animals and hunting scenes, and may have been done to please the spirits in which the tribes believed, and to bring them luck when hunting.

Yellow horse   Bull   Deer

Fishing with nets

Uro's tribe is equally good at fishing for both freshwater and saltwater fish. They spear the fish with sharply barbed harpoons or catch them in nets held down with small stones.

Beauty from the beasts

Some of these women are making necklaces from shells, animal teeth, ivory and coloured pebbles. Slices of mammoth tusk make good bracelets. The other women are preparing animal skins to make into clothes, footwear, tents, bags and bedding for the tribe.

Clues to the past

Apart from the cave paintings, the main clues to how the Cro-Magnons lived are provided by the remains of tools and weapons found in their caves. Tools made of flint, bone, antler and ivory have survived, but anything made from other materials has vanished.

Bone knife

Reaping knife

Oil lamp

Arrowheads

Fish hook

Spear-thrower

Harpoon

EARLY FARMERS

You have moved on 3000 years in time to about 10,000 B.C. when a dramatic change was taking place in the way people lived. For the first time in history people began growing their own food. This early farming took place in the fertile foothills of the Zagros Mountains in what is now Iran.

Instead of simply gathering the seeds of wild grasses to eat, they began to save some of the seed and planted it to produce a crop for the following year. This meant that they settled in one place to tend their crops and then guard the harvest once it was stored. Over the years they carefully chose and planted the seeds that would produce the best crops and began farming pulses (peas and beans) in the same way. They also began to breed sheep and goats to supply meat and milk so that they did not always have to hunt for wild animals.

People now had a new way of living. Because they were settling in one place they built permanent houses that were safer and more comfortable than tents. They no longer had to carry belongings around with them so they began to collect possessions.

Thrown to the wind
In the village they *winnow* the grain by tossing it into the air so that the *chaff* (the outer coating) blows away. They then store it in pits lined with clay or reeds to discourage theft.

Food from the land
In this scene you can see these early farmers working on the land. This year's crop is ripe, so Illa and the women harvest it to eat or store.

Daily bread
Their most important food is bread. The women grind the grain between heavy stones to make flour. They then add water and shape the mixture into round, flat loaves that they bake in clay ovens.

Harvest home
The women harvest the crop using sickles made of sharp flint blades set in wooden handles. Illa gathers ears of wheat to take to the village.

10

Breeding animals
Men look after the animals. They have successfully bred sheep and goats and even tamed the wild pigs. Taming the huge, fierce, wild cattle to produce milk proves much harder.

Handywork
The villagers make bowls and tools out of stone and weave baskets from the reeds which grow nearby. They wear clothes made from animal skins roughly sewn together.

Mud houses
This new house is nearly finished. They make the walls out of mud, gathered in special mud pits and use ladders to construct the roof from branches covered with reeds, straw and a layer of mud.

11

THE FIRST TOWN

From an early village in the Middle East you have now moved on 4000 years in time to arrive in Turkey in about 6000 B.C.. This busy and prosperous town is of great importance because it grew from a small village into the first-known town.

The town of Çatal Hüyük was successful due to trade, because its people produced items that were valued highly elsewhere. About 2000 years before,

pottery and weaving had been invented and the skilled people made pots and wove cloth from wool gathered from their sheep. They were also lucky because nearby volcanoes had produced a special volcanic glass called *obsidian* and from this they carved extremely sharp tools and even made mirrors. The people also gathered food from the wild and hunted animals for meat and skins.

A town without streets
As you can see the houses touch each other so there are no streets. To get inside you climb a ladder and drop in through a hole in the roof. Nearby Rasfa is busy trading with the villagers.

Give and take
Money has not been invented yet so people barter. This means that if one man wants a bowl, he has to offer something in exchange, perhaps a tool, that the man with the bowl agrees is of the same value. The trading can be very noisy, but good deals are made.

Fair exchange
Rasfa comes from neighbouring Syria. He wants obsidian tools and woollen cloth and has shells and good flints to trade. The townspeople need new flints but they drive a hard bargain.

Fruit and nuts
The farmers grow barley, wheat and types of peas. They also gather almonds, acorns and pistachio nuts and pick fruit, some of which they make into wine. They breed cattle and sheep and hunt wild boar and deer for meat and skins.

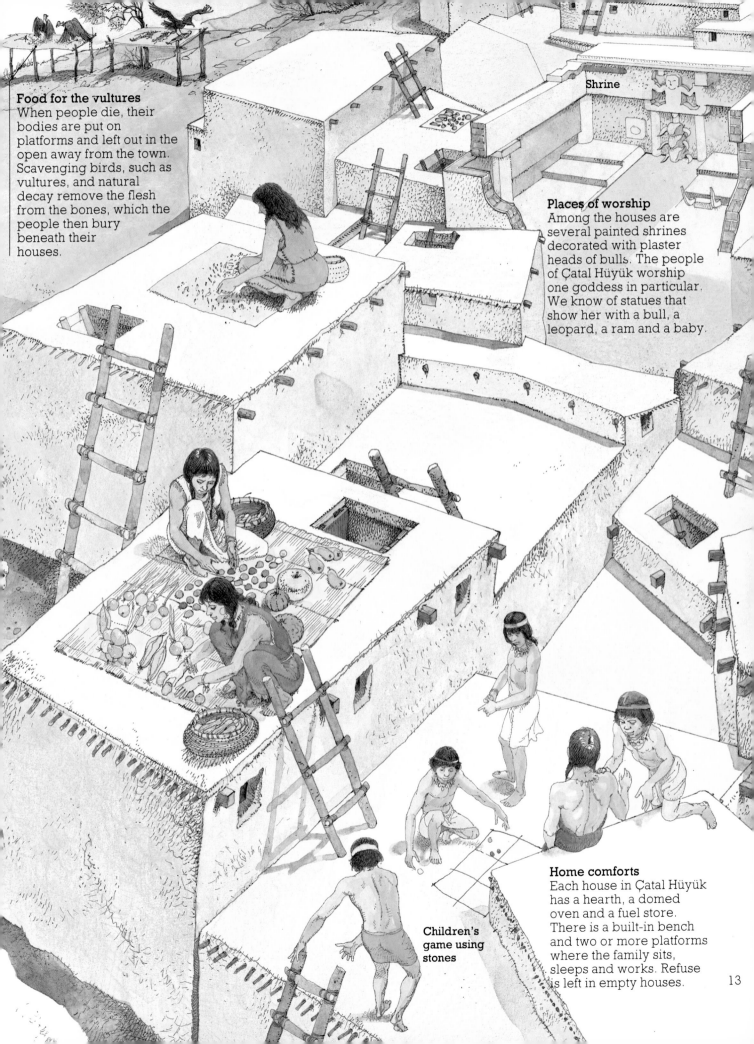

Food for the vultures
When people die, their bodies are put on platforms and left out in the open away from the town. Scavenging birds, such as vultures, and natural decay remove the flesh from the bones, which the people then bury beneath their houses.

Shrine

Places of worship
Among the houses are several painted shrines decorated with plaster heads of bulls. The people of Çatal Hüyük worship one goddess in particular. We know of statues that show her with a bull, a leopard, a ram and a baby.

Children's game using stones

Home comforts
Each house in Çatal Hüyük has a hearth, a domed oven and a fuel store. There is a built-in bench and two or more platforms where the family sits, sleeps and works. Refuse is left in empty houses.

13

THE CITY-STATES

From Turkey you have jumped south again into what is now called Iraq. You are in Sumer (Southern Mesopotamia), which is a large area of very lush country running between the River Tigris and the River Euphrates. It is about 2050 B.C., and the temperature is very hot.

Sumer was one of the earliest and greatest civilizations. Archaeological finds show us how inventive the Sumerians were: they made the first wheel, created the earliest form of writing, and were skilled artists and impressive builders.

Sumer was divided into city-states. This meant that the land and people surrounding a city were controlled by the city rulers. People had to pay taxes to the city and the city organized farms to produce successful crops, either as food or for trade. The wealth of the city-states was largely due to the invention of a new system for watering the fields, so that the fertile but dry soil could produce successful crops, even during a drought.

In the shadow of the city
On these pages you can explore the outskirts of the great city of Ur, which is in the distance. Although far away, the city controls the lives of the people who work very hard on the land.

The wheel
The Sumerians are changing the world – they have invented the wheel. The noblemen ride in chariots drawn by *onagers* (wild asses), but most people travel by boat or by foot.

Hard times
This family is worried. Last year their sheep strayed and damaged their neighbour's crops so they were fined. Now they cannot pay the taxes.

Sold into slavery
To save her family, 14-year-old Ashnan is being sold as a slave to the merchant Nesag. He has come from Ur with his servants to buy wool, cloth, grain and oil.

14

Mud and reeds
Reeds and palm trees line the river banks, so the Sumerians build their houses from sun-dried mud bricks. They make the reeds into fishermen's small boats and cow sheds.

The farmer's lot
Barley is the Sumerians' main food but they also grow a wide variety of vegetables and fruit. They raise cattle, sheep, goats, pigs and donkeys. Oxen are used to plough.

How we know
Archaeologists have excavated Sumerian buildings and found decorations inlaid in furniture, and pieces of pottery that give us an idea about everyday life.

15

THE CITY OF UR

Instead of seeing Ur from a distant village you are now in the city itself. The streets are full of people heading towards the huge temple which dominates the whole city. The mud brick temple is built on top of a *ziggurat* dedicated to the god Nanna.

The merchant Nesag
As you can see the merchants prosper in Ur. Stone, metal and good timber are in great demand. Because these materials cannot be found locally they are traded from foreign lands. The merchants barter with grain, cloth and farm produce.

Ashnan

Early bathrooms
As a wealthy man, Nesag's house has a lavatory and a system of drains. In the kitchen the slaves work on rush matting with metal tools and pottery bowls that are made locally.

Welcoming a hero
Nesag is giving a party to celebrate the safe return of his soldier-son Shulgi, who has been fighting for the king. Slaves prepare special food, and guests gather to greet their host.

A moon goddess
Geme-enlil is a priestess of the moon god Nanna. With the help of the new slave Ashnan, she is dressing to go to the temple where the king will give thanks for his great victory.

Twisting alleyways
Although Ur has some broad streets, Nesag's house is reached by many narrow alleyways. The mud brick house is built with two storeys and has a central open-air courtyard.

16

Ziggurat

Cuneiform

Off to school
Nesag's youngest son is at a school set up for the sons of prosperous parents. The pupils sit on mud benches in front of the teacher who is explaining the symbols used in Sumerian writing.

How we know
Clay tablets show us that the Sumerians invented the first writing, now called *cuneiform*. They started by scratching simple drawings into clay; in time they had a symbol for everything.

ON THE NILE

From a land divided by city-states, you have moved southwest to Egypt. The year is about 1480 B.C., and the country is united under one of a succession of powerful kings called *pharaohs*. Egypt is a great civilization and its people are highly skilled.

Egypt would be a desert if not for the River Nile that runs through it. Each summer there was the *inundation* – the Nile flooded and for several months water soaked the land. The people developed an irrigation system, as in Ur, which allowed them to farm the fertile land along the river by storing up water from this inundation. They grew wheat, barley, vegetables and flax, which they wove into fine linen cloth. The wealth of Egypt was based on its farming, its gold, and skilfully made goods which were exported.

A great nobleman's estate
It is early October and the flood is over. Neb is the steward on one of the large farms owned by Chancellor Nehsi. He has ordered the slaves to work especially hard to control the water.

Waterways
The quickest and easiest way to travel in Egypt is by water. The pharaohs travel in grand barges but noblemen fowling on the Nile and fishermen use simple boats made of local reeds called *papyrus*.

Fowling
Nehsi's birdcatchers are snaring in the reeds. The marshes are alive with water birds that are excellent to eat. Some noblemen keep a supply of birds in avaries to eat.

Flood damage
New canals and ditches carry water from the river to the fields. The banks of one of the canals has been damaged in the recent flood so Neb has sent some of the men to repair it quickly with some earth.

Canal

How we know
Noblemen in Egypt decorated their tombs with paintings of daily life so today we know how they lived. This scene shows the peasants hard at work as they reap, thresh and winnow a crop.

Boat carrying building materials

Fishing boats

Fish food
Another food supply comes from the Nile which is rich in fish. The men catch the fish with a hook and line, using a harpoon, or, as shown here, with nets slung from small boats that are rowed with oars.

Children playing games

Bursting the banks
The Nile is Egypt's only source of water. When it floods the water soaks the fields and deposits, or leaves behind from the river a layer of fertile soil called *silt*. Canals hold the water back.

Sowing seeds

October ploughing
Some men plough the fields, while others follow behind scattering seed in the *furrows* left by the plough. Animals are driven over the field to tread in the grain.

AT HOME WITH HORI

Here you can see into Hori's house. As one of the scribes working on the pharaoh's tomb, Hori is a respected and wealthy official. The house is built of sun-dried mud bricks with wooden columns and only the doorways and column bases are made of stone. Leaving the house takes you into the bustle of one of the narrow streets of Deir el Medinah, the village specially built for the various skilled craftsmen working on the pharaoh's tombs.

Deir el Medinah was part of the city of Thebes, the religious centre in the south of Egypt. The main part of the city was on the east bank of the Nile while the tombs, in the Valley of the Kings, and Deir el Medinah were on the west bank.

A Visit to Deir el Medinah
Neb's wife Merit is visiting her sister Tuya, who is married to the scribe Hori. Hori and Tuya hurry to welcome Merit into their house.

A village festival
Hori has been married before. His children are playing with friends on the roof. School is closed so that everyone can prepare for a festival tomorrow in honour of the founder of the village, Amenhotep I.

At the shrine
Tuya is going to have a baby. In ancient times this could be dangerous. Tuya spends a lot of time praying at the house shrine dedicated to her ancestors and the goddesses, who help women, such as Isis.

Inside the house
The shrine is in the front room, which Hori also uses for his work. Honoured guests like Merit are entertained in the central hall, which is higher than the other rooms with the windows at ceiling level.

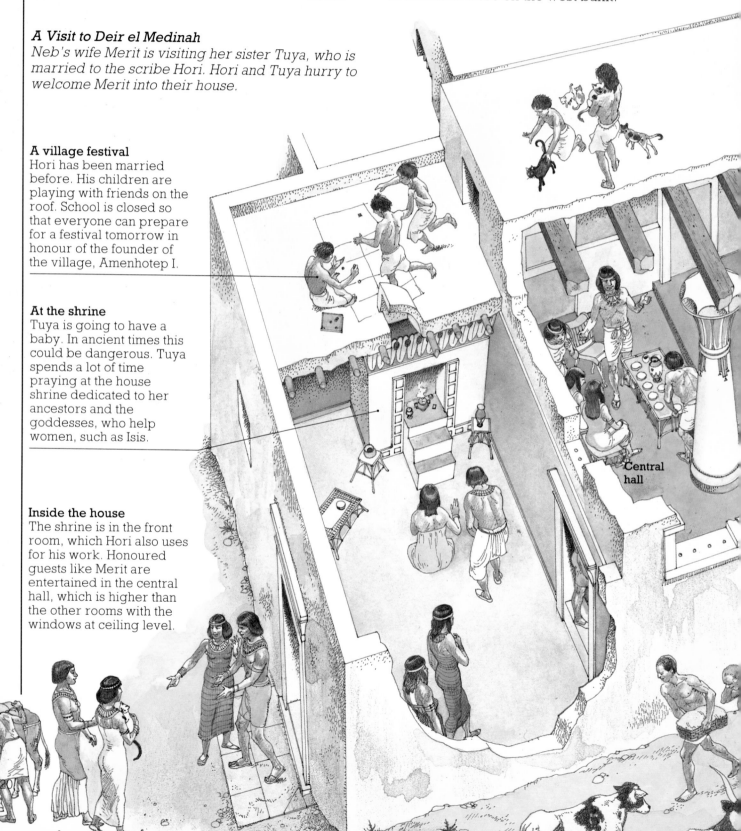

Central hall

Life on the roof
Because the houses here are small, hot and crowded, people go up on to their roofs for the breeze. They also put up awnings to shade them from the heat of the sun. In summer they may even sleep on the roof.

Slave labour
There is no such thing as money yet, and Hori is paid with goods or labour. As part of his wages he is given wine, which he keeps in the cellar, and slaves are sent to grind his grain.

Bedroom

Kitchen

Cellar

A passion for paint
The walls of the main rooms are decorated, and all the wooden furniture is painted in bright colours. There are beds, tables, chairs and stools, as well as boxes and baskets in which to store their things.

Street life
The streets are narrow, dusty and noisy. Goods and water from the Nile are carried to the village by donkey. Only the noblemen have chariots, everyone else walks. People buy their food from the small stalls.

21

THE SECRETS OF THE TOMB

The Egyptians worshipped many gods and goddesses who they believed took care of different parts of their lives. Neb lived during the New Kingdom (1567–1085 B.C.) and worshipped Amen-Re.

The Egyptians believed that a person's body remained on earth after death, but his soul, or spirit, left his body to enjoy an eternal life in the kingdom of the god Osiris, which was like a perfect

1 The mourners

Members of Hori's family surround the dead man's bed. Although the family are there, professional mourners are also hired to follow the procession to show the family's respect for their dead relative.

2 Embalming

The embalmers remove the dead man's brain and internal organs, which are put to one side. They then pack a salt called *natron* round the body to dry it out and so preserve it for the afterlife.

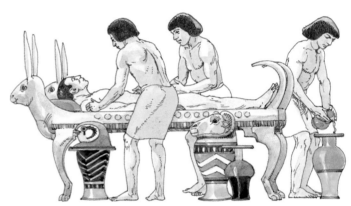

5 The procession

On the day of the funeral a procession of relatives and servants carrying the dead man's possessions walks from his house to the embalmers' workshop. There they join the priest and mourners. The mummy is now in its coffin on a sledge, followed by the *canopic chest*, which holds the internal organs.

6 "Opening the mouth"

At the door of the tomb a priest performs a rite called "Opening the Mouth," which the Egyptians believe gives the dead man control over his body again. They pray and make offerings.

7 The final farewell

They take the coffin, which is shaped like a body, down into the burial chamber and put it into a rectangular outer coffin with a wreath of flowers. Farewells are said and the lid is sealed.

Egypt. To enjoy eternal life, the Egyptians believed that the body should be preserved and placed in a tomb with its possessions. Prayers and spells ensured the soul had an endless supply of food.

A life after death
Hori's brother has just died, so here you can see how the Egyptians preserve a body for the afterlife.

3 The mummy
They then wrap the body in many metres of linen. As they wind the layers round, they place jewellery and amulets, or charms, in between the layers and pray for the man's soul.

4 Masks of the gods
They place a mask on the mummy that is a portrait of the dead man. The whole process takes seventy days, and during this time the embalmers put on animal masks and act the roles of the gods.

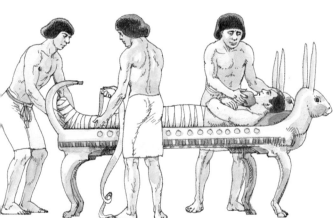

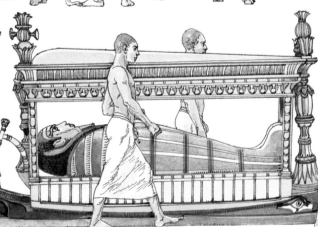

8 "Removing the Foot"
A priest sweeps the chamber where the coffin lies in the rite of "Removing the Foot". By removing any traces of human life, the Egyptians believe they can keep evil away from the tomb.

9 The Judgement Hall
A funeral feast is over. By now the man's soul is being weighed against a feather in the Judgement Hall of Osiris. He has led a good life so they balance and his reward is a peaceful and eternal life.

THE WEALTH OF THE SEA KING

It is still the same time, 1480 B.C., but you have followed the River Nile north into the Mediterranean Sea, to arrive on the rocky island of Crete in the blazing sunshine.

The Cretans were farmers and sailors whose island had been free from invasion for centuries. As a result, the civilization that grew up was unique. They even developed their own script, which is

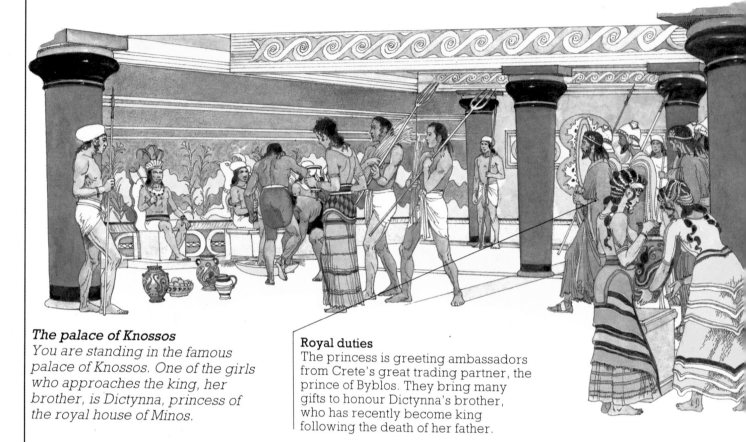

The palace of Knossos
You are standing in the famous palace of Knossos. One of the girls who approaches the king, her brother, is Dictynna, princess of the royal house of Minos.

Royal duties
The princess is greeting ambassadors from Crete's great trading partner, the prince of Byblos. They bring many gifts to honour Dictynna's brother, who has recently become king following the death of her father.

Bull-leaping (*below*)
The visitors are most impressed by the bull-leapers. These young men and girls risk their lives vaulting between the horns of charging bulls in the palace courtyard. It is done to honour the gods and for excitement. Artists use it as a theme for some of the rich *frescoes*, or wall paintings, which decorate the palace.

A stone goddess (*right*)
At her private shrine in the palace Dictynna makes offerings of flowers, food and wine, and prays each day. Following the fashion of the woman attending court, the statuette of the goddess wears a flounced, bell-shaped skirt beneath a tight bodice, and her hair is arranged in long curls. In her hands she holds two vipers.

now called "Linear A". The Cretans were great builders and craftsmen who produced beautiful pottery and other goods, which they traded for metal and precious stones. They also produced grain, olives, fruit and wine, which were stored in the palaces for export or payment to craftsmen. Crete was ruled by a succession of kings who organized the people from the palaces.

Sea creatures
The Cretans love the sea which gives them fish to eat and wealth from trade. This is shown in the lively fish and other sea creatures that they painted on their walls or pottery.

Clean living
Knossos has a complicated drainage system to carry away water from the spring and autumn rains. The Cretans consider cleanliness to be very important, and so the palaces are well supplied with bathrooms.

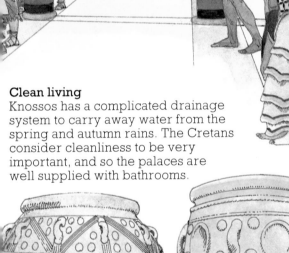

Stored in jars (*above*)
Knossos was excavated by archaeologists. In the maze of large storerooms beneath the palace they found, still in place, many of the enormous jars that once held farm produce waiting to be traded.

Religion outdoors (*below*)
Besides the private shrines in palaces and houses, the Cretans also worshipped in caves and on mountainsides. Cretan rings and seals, which stamped designs on clay or wax, show scenes of a goddess with her priestesses and the Sacred Double Axe, or with a young god or animals.

INVADERS FROM THE NORTH

From Crete you have followed the Adriatic Sea to reach the north of Italy, and then travelled west into France. You have arrived in the year 500 B.C., when this part of central Europe is called Gaul.

Gaul was the homeland of a fierce, warring race of people called Celts. The Greeks and Romans saw them as "barbarians", or uncivilized foreigners, but treated them with understandable caution and respected their bravery in battle.

The Celts were settled around 700 B.C. in Hallstadt, West Germany, and from there they spread west through France and Spain, and north into Holland and Britain. They also went south into Italy, where they defeated the city of Rome in 385 B.C., and the city of Delphi, in Greece, about a century later. As the Romans' empire expanded (see page 40), they slowly conquered all the Celtic lands, except for Ireland and parts of Scotland, but not without resistance.

The Hallstadt Celts lived in tribes in organized villages. They were skilled metal smiths and prospered by trading and mining valuable salt.

A family of metal workers
Kai lives in a large village in central Gaul. Because his family have always been metal smiths, they are highly respected by the tribe and have a large and well-equipped hut.

Fenced in
Kai's village belongs to the chief of the tribe, who controls the area. The tribe defend their village by encircling the timber and thatch huts with a *palisade*, a tall wooden fence, and a deep ditch.

Storage jar

Grinding corn

Raiders!
The tribe lives under a constant threat from raiders, who steal cattle from the chief's territory. But the Celts are prepared; armed with spears and shields, they can pursue the raiders on foot or in horse-drawn chariots.

A fair description
The Greek writers describe the Celts as being tall, fair and keen to display their battle honours by wearing elaborate armour and weapons. Their famous quick-tempers and excitable natures cause a great deal of fighting.

From power to ploughs
Below the chief and his family are the nobles, who are usually warriors, the *druids* (holy men), the craftsmen and then the people. Most Celts are farmers and they use cattle to pull their special iron-tipped ploughs.

All dressed up
Using an iron cooking pot over the fire, Kai's mother helps to prepare a feast to welcome some Greek traders from a colony in the south. To mark the event, they dress in brightly coloured woollen clothes, woven in patterns.

Weaving

Bedrooms

Forging ahead

You have walked out of Kai's hut and from where you stand you can see the metal smiths hard at work. Kai knows his ancestors were among the first people to extract ore from rocks by using great heat, and then, by mixing different metals, produce bronze. He is proud of his family history and longs to be as skilled as his father.

Emergency builders

The hut belonging to Kai's uncle was destroyed when it caught fire. The villagers help to rebuild it. Men on the ground prepare mud for the walls and a couple are binding together bundles of straw to be fixed into the wooden framework of the roof.

Men of iron

The Celts not only use iron to make tools and weapons, but they also use gold and bronze to make fine jewellery, decorative armour and containers. All these beautiful items are highly valued for trade.

A gift to the goddess

After an attack the Celts gather up the enemy's armour and give it to a druid. Adding some new pieces, made by Kai's family, the druid throws it into the river. This is done to thank the tribe's mother-goddess for victory.

Fear of attack

Kai envies the warriors who triumphantly return from battle, boasting of their deeds. But in spite of their victories, the chief knows that the village needs better protection than a fence. He wants to build a hill fort for the tribe.

How we know

Due to decay, there are very few everyday objects, such as baskets, leatherwork and cloth, and no written language, for us to study. Only the holes left by the central poles of the huts remain for the archaeologists to discover. The hill forts, however, are impressive because the earthworks, great excavations of land surrounding a fortified village, look like huge steps cut into a hill.

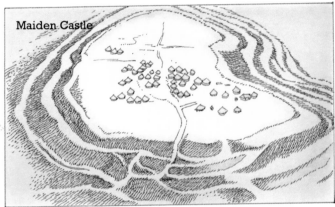

Maiden Castle

Armed to the teeth

Long swords, daggers and spears are the warriors' favourite weapons. Their wild bravery, coupled with the strength of their new iron weapons, make them frightening opponents. Apart from armour for battle, they also have magnificently decorated pieces for display only, and excellent tools. The men also use slings as weapons.

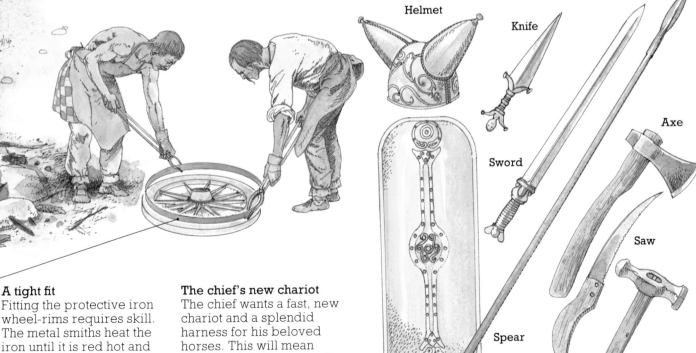

Helmet

Knife

Sword

Axe

Saw

Spear

Hammer

Shield

A tight fit

Fitting the protective iron wheel-rims requires skill. The metal smiths heat the iron until it is red hot and position it round the wheel using tongs. They then pour water over the iron, and as it cools it shrinks into place.

The chief's new chariot

The chief wants a fast, new chariot and a splendid harness for his beloved horses. This will mean work for the carpenter, the leatherworkers and the village smiths. Chariots are made of wood, but the wheel-rims are iron.

29

HERDSMEN OF SIBERIA

From Gaul you have travelled thousands of miles east to an area that is now called Siberia. The date is 500 B.C., and for miles around are the vast expanses of treeless plains and snow-capped mountains now known as the Steppes.

Instead of farming, the tribes that lived in the harsh conditions of Siberia were nomadic, constantly moving their families and animals around in search of new pastures.

Rather than hunting the wild horses that lived on the Steppes for meat, these nomadic tribes caught and tamed them. They then rode the horses at great speed, rounding up entire herds of horses that they sold or used for carrying loads and providing milk.

The horsemen were frightening warriors. They were highly skilled archers and greatly feared by the Chinese, Persians and Greeks, who also noted their excellence with horses. The nomadic metal smiths produced fine ornaments, and the women made intricately sewn designs.

The horsemen of the Altai Mountains
You have joined a tribe of herdsmen from the west of Siberia. Rudek, the chief, and his men have herded the horses back home.

Away from home
At certain times of the year, the men round up the wild horses and herd them to distant pastures where the grazing is better. The herdsmen sleep in felt or birch-bark tents while they are far from home.

Food and fodder
The herdsmen hunt wild deer for meat, but they also breed sheep, some cattle and chickens. The only crop is hay, which they grow as *fodder*, food stored to feed the animals during the winter.

Horse-play
The tribesmen are proud of their horses. On special occasions Rudek puts a brightly embroidered saddle on his horse, plaits its tail and fits decorations that look like reindeer antlers to its head.

Settling down

When the herdsmen return, they join their families in a settlement of houses made of logs, with bark roofs. Inside the women make *appliqués*, by sewing shapes of material on to a background.

Making leather

How we know

These people had no written language, so much of our knowledge about them comes from tombs discovered at Pazyryk in the Steppes. The people were buried deep in a log-lined pit covered with stones. With them were their horses and possessions. A few years later the tombs were robbed, allowing water to seep in. It then froze and preserved the tomb's contents.

Skin-deep

The tribesmen's clothes are made of linen, wool, fur and leather, to keep them warm. They love lavish embroidery and gold ornaments. Rudek has *tattoos*, like drawings, stained into his skin.

Pots and pans

The tribesmen have low wooden tables with oval tops and carved legs, and sit on stools or cushions. Stone oil lamps provide light. They use leather, clay and wooden bowls, and copper cauldrons.

LIFE IN ANCIENT GREECE

So little is known about what happened in Greece in the years 1000–800 B.C., that the period is called the "Greek Dark Ages". But now it is about 424 B.C., and you have arrived in the magnificent city of Athens.

In the 400 years or so after the Dark Ages, Greece grew into one of the greatest civilizations in history. It produced some of the best playwrights and philosophers, or thinkers, ever known, and the *classical* style of its architecture and statues was copied for many centuries in Europe.

Lysander

An early start
Lysander is 12 years old. This year his father is a city official, chosen by fellow citizens. Because Amyntas is wealthy, he has been able to pay for Lysander to go to school from the earliest age, at seven years old. A slave helps the sleepy Lysander.

Plans over breakfast
Lysander has a quick breakfast of bread, cheese and olives. He plans to sneak off to see his father speak at the Assembly of Citizens, which meets three or four times a month. Today they will be discussing new peace proposals for the states.

Family prayers
Everyday, before leaving the house, the family meets for prayers round the altar in the courtyard. Today Philip, Lysander's elder brother, is setting out to fight in the wars between Athens and Sparta, so they ask the goddess Athene for help.

Thea

Getting dressed
Thea, Lysander's 10-year-old sister, is washing under a waterspout in the villa before dressing. She normally wears a *chiton*, a simple robe made of a piece of linen (or wool in winter) sewn together down the side, but left open at the top.

Homework
Like other girls, Thea does not go to school. Instead, her mother teaches her the various skills expected of a wife, in preparation for when she is married. By that time, she must be able to run a large household and organize the slaves and food bills.

Going out
Because she comes from a good family, Thea spends most of her time at home. She occasionally visits friends and accompanies her mother to the temples on festival days. Each temple is dedicated to one of many Greek gods or goddesses.

Ancient Greece was divided into city-states and rivalries developed between the strong states, such as Athens and Sparta. Each state had its own rulers, but in Athens there was a *democracy*, where the citizens elected their leaders. All men were citizens, but not women, children or slaves.

Just an ordinary day
Lysander, Alexander and Thea are the children of Amyntas and Campaspne. Here you can see how they spend a typical day in their home town, Athens.

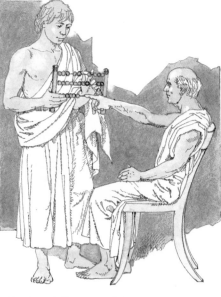

Wax works
Lysander has his own slave who takes him to school and stays with him to make sure he works. The boys write with a pointed *stylus* on wooden tablets covered with wax. When the tablets are full, they just smooth over the wax and start again.

Early adding machines
To help with their sums, each pupil has an *abacus*. This is a wooden frame that has wires strung across it, threaded with beads. The boys study many subjects: the works of the famous Greek poets and playwrights, music and history.

Budding athletes
Athletics takes up part of each day. Lysander practises running, jumping, boxing and wrestling. He excels at throwing the *discus*, (a plate-shaped piece of copper) and the spear-shaped javelin. Every four years he visits the Olympic Games.

Alexander

Discussion group
Alexander is the second son of the family. He is 17 and left school two years ago. Now he is attending classes on public speaking and takes part in discussion groups that are conducted by one of the city's leading philosophers.

The theatre
Alexander is stage-struck. After seeing a play by Euripides, he wants to write his own play. The theatres are open-air and audiences sit in seats that are cut out of a hillside and arranged in a circle around the stage. All the actors wear masks.

Military training
Next year Alexander will come of age and will be considered a citizen. All young men are taught from boyhood to be soldiers, and Alexander must now do two years' military service. He practises with a sword, shield and spear.

LYSANDER'S HOME

It is early evening of the following day and you are in the family's large house in Athens.

Paintings, statues and *relief sculptures* (pictures carved or modelled out of the surface of a flat piece of stone or clay), give us a clue today about how the Greeks lived at home. Most large houses in Athens were built out of sun-dried bricks, on a carefully levelled stone base. The wooden-framed roof was covered with overlapping tiles. The public rooms and kitchen were on the ground floor, with the private quarters and bedrooms above. At the centre of the house was a courtyard, in which stood the family altar. A wooden staircase led from the courtyard to the upper storey. Wealthy families had wells, but most people fetched water in large pottery jars from public fountains.

Night lights
In the bedroom, a slave is putting a chiton into the storage chest. Behind her are the wooden couches with covers and pillows for sleeping on, and a tall holder for an oil lamp.

The dinner party
Amyntas is giving a dinner party for friends because he wants to talk about business. They lie on couches, eating from a low table. The women never join the men to eat.

Folding furniture
The furniture is wooden or bronze, sometimes inlaid with precious metals and ivory, and they use folding leather stools and chairs. They store their clothes in large baskets or chests.

The altar
The Greeks believe in many gods and goddesses and over the years they have built up legends around them. The father of the gods is Zeus, who lives on Mount Olympus.

A full house

Lysander's family is scattered throughout the house. It is early evening and the slaves are preparing food in the kitchen, or weaving cloth in the room above. The noisiest place is the room rented by the potter.

How we know

We get a lot of information about everyday life from the paintings on their pottery. There are two famous kinds of pottery – "black figure ware" and "red figure ware". The size and shape of the vases varies greatly.

The heart of the house

The courtyard is always busy. Campaspne protects herself from the sun, while she sits with her children. A messenger bursts in with news from Philip – Athens has been defeated.

Women's work

Several slaves have been bought for their spinning and weaving skills. As well as making woollen and linen cloth to make clothes for the family, they weave patterned wall-hangings.

A slave's freedom

The slaves are cooking meat and vegetables over a charcoal fire. They bake the bread in ovens. Household slaves earn tips and sometimes save enough to buy their freedom.

Pots of money

Amyntas owns several farms, and he makes money from selling the farm produce. But recently he has been unable to pay the high taxes, so he rents a room to a potter.

MARKET DAY IN ATHENS

A few days have passed, and you have walked a short distance from Lysander's house, through the crowded streets to the marketplace or *agora*.

In Athens, as in other Greek cities, some craftsmen sold their wares directly from their workshops, but most people did their shopping in the agora. People set up stalls in the open area of the agora, and under the shade of the *stoa*. This was a long, two-storeyed building, one side of which was open and supported by columns. The citizens also went there to buy slaves and hire workmen and used it as a meeting place. Men often did the shopping; if they were rich they took slaves to carry the purchases. In Athens officials checked the quality of the goods and ensured that the sellers used accurate scales or measures.

Shopping around
The owners of the market stalls are busy trading. All around you, goods and money are changing hands and people are exchanging ideas and gossip.

Banking
Because everyone now uses money, banks are necessary. In the market place bankers will lend money to most people. But, like the moneychangers, they charge a fee.

Oil for washing
Everyone buys olive oil for cooking. They also burn it in lamps, and use it instead of soap – rubbing it over their bodies and then scraping it off, along with the dirt.

An expensive butcher
Farmers breed goats, pigs, chickens and, less often, sheep for meat. They sell it in the market, but only the rich can afford meat. Most people eat fish, eggs, fruit and vegetables.

Choosing fabrics
Most people buy material in the market. They usually choose plain linen or wool, and save brightly coloured clothes for very special occasions. The Greeks also import silk from the East.

How we know
Today we have many Greek coins to study. The most common shape is a circle of metal with a symbol, or picture, of the city's chief god or goddess. Later coins are stamped with the portraits of city rulers.

From barter to money
Instead of bartering, the Greeks use pieces of metal that have been stamped by the city officials as a guarantee of their value. Such coins were invented around 600 B.C. by the Greek colony of Lydia, in Turkey.

Money changing
Because each city has its own coinage, people have to exchange their money when visiting another city, if they want to spend any money. There are moneychangers in the agora, who charge a fee for this service.

Agora

A sweet tooth
Lysander tries to persuade Amyntas to buy something sweet. The Greeks do not have sugar so they sweeten their food with honey. The beekeepers use special pottery hives.

The tavern
Alexander spends a lot of his time drinking wine with friends in the *taverna*, a popular meeting place for men. The wine, made from local grapes, is stored in pottery jars.

37

A VISIT TO CHINA

You have travelled east for thousands of miles and arrive in China. It is around 130 B.C. and the Han Dynasty, or family of rulers, is in power.

An independent and major civilization grew up in the huge country of China. Its great cities produced inventive craftsmen, ingenious writers and thinkers, and established carefully ordered societies that deeply honoured their ancestors.

By around 5000 B.C., the people farmed millet, soya beans and later rice, and bred dogs and pigs. They also bred silkworms, having discovered that these caterpillars produced a thread that could be finely woven. After 1500 B.C., during the Shang Dynasty, they created a system of writing and invented a method for casting bronze. Following two centuries of civil war, the country was united under the Emperor of Ch'in, which gave China its name. The Ch'in Emperors began major work on the massive Great Wall, built to defend the northern border. In 206 B.C. the Han Dynasty seized power.

The Lady Ch'eng
These pages show the palace of Lady Ch'eng, consort of the Han Emperor Ching, just before she is taken ill and dies.

Home sweet home
The people's houses are wooden and they paint the thin walls with lacquer as waterproofing. Often the houses have two storeys, and watchtowers so that a lookout can give an early warning of any attacking invaders.

How we know
When Lady Ch'eng dies her tomb is sealed with thick layers of clay and charcoal to preserve it.

A box of cosmetics
Perfectly preserved in the tomb is a box painted with *lacquer*, a glossy paint made from tree resin. A silk scarf and mittens are in the top of the box, and in a number of smaller boxes below there are brushes, combs and cosmetics.

Servants for eternity
In earlier dynasties, the Chinese killed servants and buried them with their dead masters or mistresses to serve them in a life after death, or so they believed. Lady Ch'eng is buried with wooden or clay models of her servants.

Bitter medicines
Lady Ch'eng is about fifty. She wears a hairpiece and is rather stout. In recent years she has had problems with a weak heart and her doctors have prescribed different medicines. She takes cinnamon, peppercorns and ground magnolia bark.

A gift horse
Lady Ch'eng rests by the pool as she waits to see a horse that the Emperor has given one of their sons. It was brought from the west, so it is larger and swifter than a Chinese horse. Only the rich can afford horses and travel in carriages.

A painted palace
The palace, also wooden, has several storeys and is richly decorated inside with paintings and finely worked bronze ornaments. The beautiful grounds that surround the palace, contain decorative ponds and an ornamental house.

Miniature houses
Tombs often contain models of different types of houses, made of intricately worked bronze or pottery. Some of these have their own courtyards containing wells, and farm houses have model animals and granaries for storage.

Covered in silk
Silk garments and lengths of silk are buried with Lady Ch'eng. One dress is so fine that it weighs almost nothing. Her shoes, stockings and mittens are also silk. Some items are plain, but others are painted and embroidered.

39

ROMAN FAMILY LIFE

You have travelled far west again, to arrive back in Europe. Your new location is a boot-shaped country called Italy. It is about 20 B.C. and you are in the countryside around Ancient Rome.

From a settlement around the River Tiber, Rome grew into one of the most successful empires in history. At the height of its power it controlled the whole of Italy and vast areas of land that extended

Caius Claudius Sabinus

On these pages you can see into the villa, *or country house, belonging to Claudius, a wealthy senator.*

Heated floors

At the centre of the villa there is an *atrium*, or open-air courtyard. All the rooms in the front open off this, and in the middle of this a pool catches valuable rainwater. Under the house is a heating system called a *hypocaust*.

Painted walls

The walls are decorated with frescoes, or wall-paintings, as in Crete, and the lower rooms are paved with marble. Claudius wants a *mosaic* floor, made from tiny pieces of inlaid stone, and he also wants to buy a new marble statue.

Reflected glory

Bedrooms are on the first floor. Paulina is the wife of Claudius's son, Marcus. Two slaves arrange her hair in fashionable curls while she looks at the result in a silver mirror. Her fine jewellery is made of gold and precious gems.

Match-making

Julia, Claudius's wife, is seated on a couch, talking to Senator Vitellius and his wife, Tullia. They are planning a marriage between their son, who is in the army, and Julia's daughter. The young couple talk in the atrium.

Lavatory

north into England and south into Egypt.

Rome was a *republic* where the people, who were citizens as in Athens, elected two heads of state, called *consuls*. The consuls were advised by a group of men called *senators*, who were chosen from leading Roman families. But in 27 B.C., after vicious civil wars, a man called Octavian seized power and became the first emperor of Rome.

School-time
Because Claudius is rich, he does not send his son, Julius, to school, but employs a Greek freedman as tutor. Girls rarely attend lessons, but Livia joins her brother as the teacher reads from a scroll of papyrus, or *volumen*.

The eldest son
Claudius is in the study with Marcus, his eldest son. Claudius is liked by Octavian, who is now Emperor Augustus, so he is optimistic about his son's career. Marcus has had a good training as a *tribune*, or officer, in the army.

Garden

Shrine

Atrium

THE JOURNEY BACK TO ROME

You have joined Claudius and his family as they return to their town house in Rome. The new road stretches in a straight line towards the city.

As Rome expanded its empire, armies needed to move further and faster, so they built thousands of miles of roads to help the men move more quickly. In 146 B.C., after many years of fighting, the Roman army conquered Greece. The Romans learnt a great deal from the Greeks and adopted many of their ideas. They copied Greek art and architecture and used Greek engineering skills in warfare and building. The Romans added to these skills by inventing a concrete-like material that made their buildings stronger, and so allowed them to build more daring structures, such as arches.

All roads lead to Rome
These pages show how Claudius's family travels. They usually take an armed escort, despite the army, because bandits sometimes attack and rob travellers.

Building bridges
Slaves, who do the building in Rome, are constructing arches around a wooden frame, which they will remove once the bridge is secure. They use wooden cranes to lift the stones.

Family travel
The women travel in *litters*, which are like carriages without wheels carried by slaves. Marcus takes Julius in his chariot and Claudius rides his favourite horse.
They pass carriages, carts and wagons, as well as people on foot.

Litter

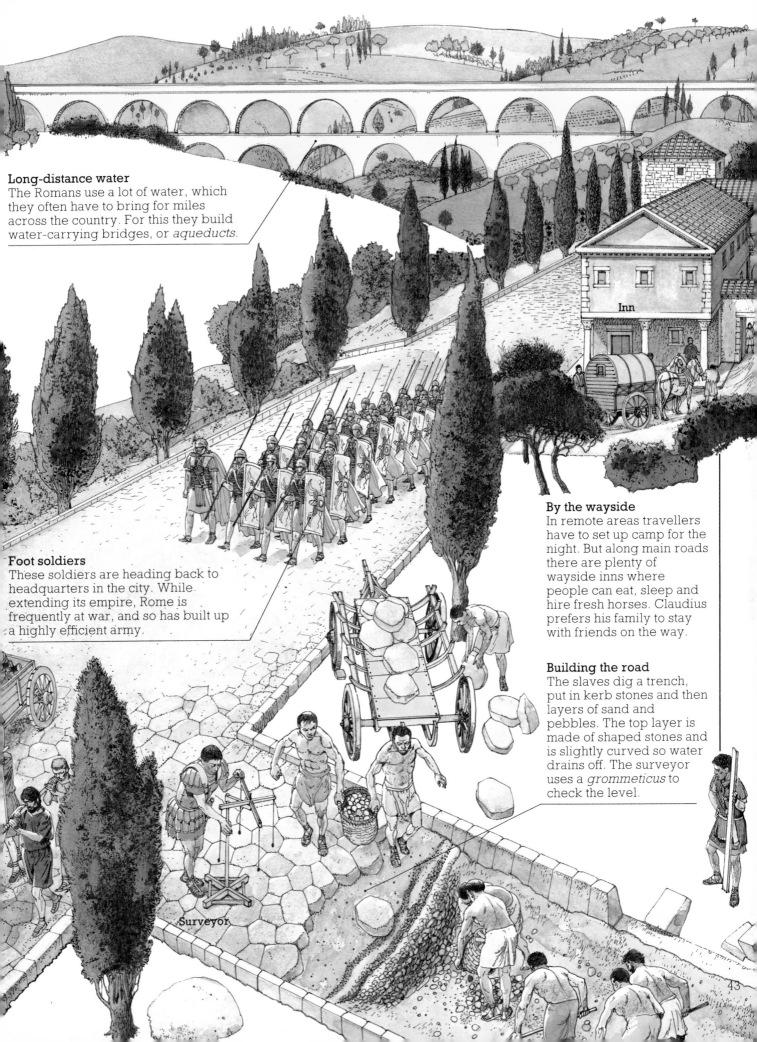

Long-distance water
The Romans use a lot of water, which they often have to bring for miles across the country. For this they build water-carrying bridges, or *aqueducts*.

Inn

Foot soldiers
These soldiers are heading back to headquarters in the city. While extending its empire, Rome is frequently at war, and so has built up a highly efficient army.

By the wayside
In remote areas travellers have to set up camp for the night. But along main roads there are plenty of wayside inns where people can eat, sleep and hire fresh horses. Claudius prefers his family to stay with friends on the way.

Building the road
The slaves dig a trench, put in kerb stones and then layers of sand and pebbles. The top layer is made of shaped stones and is slightly curved so water drains off. The surveyor uses a *grommeticus* to check the level.

Surveyor

43

A ROMAN STREET SCENE

After your journey from the villa, you have stopped not at Claudius's house, but in a much poorer part of Rome, where the tradesmen, craftsmen and less prosperous people live.

Most Romans did not come from rich families, and although all men were citizens (excluding slaves or foreigners), few of them had much money and most of them lived in badly built, wooden-framed flats above shops. There were not enough jobs, so Roman officials organized free grain for the unemployed and arranged the games, chariot races, and built splendid public baths.

The street life
Here you can see the people and houses in the poorer part of Rome. Marcus's new job is to collect taxes from them.

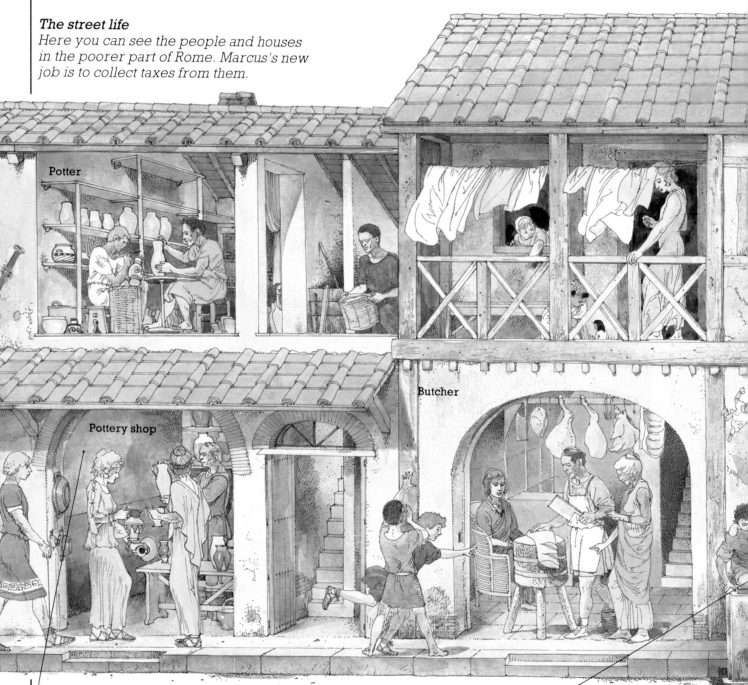

Potter

Pottery shop

Butcher

Stop thief!
The shops open on to the pavement and have their counters at the front. At night the tradesmen fit wooden shutters across the shops, which they lock to discourage thieves.

Up in flames
In the poorer parts of the city the overcrowded buildings sometimes fall down, killing the people inside. Fires are common, so there are watchmen and a fire-fighting force.

Public lavatories
The more expensive, ground floor flats have private lavatories that are connected to the main sewers. However, most people use the public lavatories on every street.

Running water
Most flat-dwellers fetch their drinking water from the stone public fountains, on every street. They have to pay officials to have water piped directly into their homes.

44

Making scrolls

Olive oil
shop

Baker

Barber

Rooms to let
Very few people can
afford houses; most of
them live in apartment
blocks, or flats, and rent
one or more rooms. A few
flats are comfortable, but
most are in need of repair.

Shops
The flats are built around
small courtyards and many
people rent our their front
rooms to small businesses
or shops like potters or
barbers. Many people also
work in the courtyards.

Food and drink
Few of the flats have
kitchens, so most people
buy cooked food. There
are bakers, and other
shops sell olive oil, wine
and hot food. Vegetables
are sold in the market.

The sewers
Clay sewage pipes run
from the lavatories to a
system of pipes under the
pavements. These pipes
then join the main tunnels
that carry all the waste into
the River Tiber.

A DAY WITH CLAUDIUS

You have left the poorer area of Rome to join Senator Claudius, who mixes pleasure with work.

Senators came from a group of people who were at the top of Roman society. Beneath them were the *equites*, who were successful men involved in business. The largest group of people were the poorest, or *plebeians*. All free men were citizens and could wear a *toga*, a large piece of cloth wrapped around the body, as a symbol of their citizenship. Women were in a weak position, as the

1 The family shrine

Every morning Claudius leads the prayers as the whole family gathers round the shrine in the atrium. The shrine holds figures of the *lares* and *penates*, the guardian spirits of the house and family. The family also prays to Vesta, goddess of the hearth, who protects the household. Julia is faithful to the Egyptian goddess Isis.

2 Public baths

Although he has a perfectly good suite of baths in his town house, Claudius often chooses to go to the public baths because he can meet friends and do business with colleagues. Today he takes Marcus along. After leaving their clothes in the changing room, they sit in the "hot room" where boiling water gives off steam to make them sweat.

5 The library

Claudius goes home to his library. He should be preparing his speech for the next meeting of the Senate, but a bookseller has just delivered a copy of a new work on philosophy and he cannot resist starting it. The book is a series of scrolls, made of Egyptian papyrus. Like all Roman books, it is hand copied, usually by a Greek slave, from another book.

6 The Senate

Claudius makes a point of attending every meeting at the Senate, even though the Senate has less control of Rome, since the Emperor seized power. Today it is a meeting to investigate the case of one of its own members who commands one of the provinces, a large area held by the Empire. He has been accused of overtaxing the people.

men in their family, whether the husband, father or son, had authority over them, although divorce was possible. In addition there was a mass of slaves, captured as Rome extended its empire. A rich man might have as many as a hundred slaves.

Business and pleasure
Here you can see that Claudius has a full day. But between his business and his duties as senator, he enjoys life.

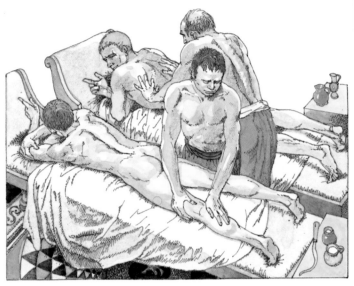

3 A dip in the pool
Claudius and Marcus now pass through the hot and warm water-baths, and finally swim in the cold water pool. They talk to friends and later on have a light meal. Women have their own set of rooms at the baths. A good baths, like this one, offers food, barbers, beauty treatments, a garden, a library and an area for athletic exercise.

4 Secret worries
After bathing, Claudius and Marcus have a massage. It is a good opportunity to talk, but Marcus is silent as he is worried about his wife spending money. Paulina has gone in her litter to the Forum, Rome's market-place, where she wants to buy some Oriental silk. Marcus is already in debt, from betting on the chariot races and playing dice.

7 Bloodthirsty sports
Games are held in honour of the emperor's birthday and huge crowds of Romans go to the Colosseum, a massive theatre without a stage, where the games are held. Most Romans are excited by watching the *gladiators*, prisoners who are trained to fight to the death. But Julia does not enjoy it and leaves before the rest of the crowd.

8 The dinner party
In the evening Claudius and Julia give a party to celebrate the Emperor's birthday. The guests lie on couches, helping themselves to the food with spoons and their fingers. The dishes include such delicacies as stuffed dormice, roast ostrich and exotic fruit, washed down with wine drunk from glass goblets. Poets and musicians entertain.

47

AT HOME WITH THE VIKINGS

You have left the luxuries of Rome behind you travelled north through what are now Switzerland and Germany, and crossed the icy North Sea into Norway. The journey has carried you forward in time to A.D. 950. In the meantime, the Roman Empire has collapsed and Christianity has spread to Europe.

Like Sweden, Denmark and parts of Finland, the land we now know as Norway was populated by the Norsemen, a tough race of farmers, traders and fishermen. But they were better known as warriors and adventurers. By the end of the eighth century A.D., the Norsemen had set out in sturdy boats and reached many parts of central Europe, where they looted, destroyed and killed. Monks described the raiders' bloodstained progress in *chronicles* (like diaries), rulers offered fortunes in return for safety, and everyone prayed to be delivered from the Norsemen, whom they called Vikings.

Eric the blacksmith's village
On these pages you can discover a Viking village, situated at the end of a fjord (a long inlet from the sea) where Eric is the chief's blacksmith.

Many farmhands
Eric works for the chief, Gorm One-Eye. Gorm, the members of his large family and their followers, farm the land, but a lot of the work is done by slaves, who were captured in a recent raid abroad.

Cow shed

Bedroom

Houses like barns
A forest stretches between the village and the distant mountains, so timber is plentiful. The houses are timber-framed with wooden or stone walls, and the roofs are thatched.

A lack of privacy
The houses usually have one windowless room where everybody sleeps and eats. The women cook on a central hearth, and smoke escapes through a hole in the roof.

Surviving the winter
The villagers have to store food indoors to last all winter. They cannot feed all their animals during the winter, so they kill some and smoke and salt the meat to preserve it.

No spare room
Even in the summer months the houses are full of flour and other food stored in large barrels. The rest of the space is taken up with wooden beds and benches.

48

Ploughing

Sowing seeds

Weapons for warriors
Gorm respects Eric for his skill with bronze and iron. He makes expert double-sided swords, and flat, curve-edged blades for the *broad axes* that are used by the warriors.

Blacksmith

Making charcoal

Storehouse

Drying fish

A choice of food
The grain crop is vital because they make it into bread, beer and porridge. They grow vegetables, gather fruit and make honey. But they have to trade for supplies of salt.

Fish and fowl
The Vikings breed cattle, sheep, goats and pigs to provide them with meat, milk, wool and leather, and have chickens and geese. They also hunt for meat and eat masses of fish.

49

Wandering seamen

You have now walked to the harbour where people are loading up one ship, and building another.

The Vikings are inspired shipbuilders. Using local timber, usually oak, they build knorrs, sturdy boats for fishing trips or local trading, and longships, warships used for raiding. By following the sun, stars and any landmarks, they navigate across vast expanses of sea.

Boat shelter

Warrior-turned-trader
Since Gorm lost an eye he concentrates on trading. The villagers load up one of the knorrs with farm produce, and some metalwork for trade.

Knorr

All hands on deck
The Viking ships can sail on rivers or at sea. There is an oar-shaped wooden rudder for steering and a large square sail, but the men often row into and out of harbour.

Ship-shape
The shipbuilders create the boat's curved outline by first soaking the wood to make it pliable. The *keel*, a wooden strip attached underneath the boat gives it stability.

How we know
Archaeological remains and chronicles help us to imagine the Vikings' way of life. But more exciting are the actual ships that have been found. The Viking tradition of burying their warriors in ships under a mound of earth means that there are marvellous remains to study today, such as the ships found in Gokstad and Oseberg, in Norway. Also, five ships, sunk by the Vikings to block a channel in the Norwegian Roskilde Fjord, have been preserved in mud.

Buried ship

Favourite ports
Gorm and his men often sail to Dublin, an Irish port, or to Sweden where, in the great port of Birka, there are visiting Arabs who are eager to trade for furs, slaves and precious lumps of amber.

Beastly carvings
Viking carvings in wood and stone often depict animals or intricate patterns. The craftsmen carve swirls or the heads of beasts on the front extensions, or *prows*, of their longships.

Viking boat-houses
The villagers have small rowing boats in which they catch fish from the fjords, or even compete in rowing races for pleasure. When not in use, they keep their boats in thatched shelters.

A god of thunder
The Vikings worship many gods and goddesses. The father of their gods is Odin, god of wisdom and battle. They also place great faith in Thor, who rules the weather.

MEDIEVAL ENGLAND

After a voyage south you find yourself in a small English village in about A.D. 1320. This date means that you have arrived during the Middle Ages, also called the medieval period, which lasted from around A.D. 1000–1450.

When William the Conqueror invaded England in A.D. 1066 he introduced a way of organizing the people that had developed in his homeland, in what is now France. This system, known as the *feudal* system, ensured that every community was run by a knight who would be able to defend the area if necessary. It worked like this: the English king gave his nobles large areas of land in return for the nobles' oath of loyalty and a number of soldiers; the nobles in turn allowed the knights to use this land, and as payment, the knights offered themselves to the nobles as soldiers required by the king. The peasants living on the *manors*, the knights' land, worked for their overlords the knights, in return for protection.

Within four walls
Here you can see inside the house belonging to Agnes and Fulk. It looks rather crowded, but compared to many other peasants, they are fortunate.

Ploughing

Sheep pen

Milking a cow

Hard-working peasants
Some peasants are *freemen*, who only pay rent for their land, but most are *villeins* like Fulk. This means they have to pay money to their overlord, usually a knight, and work on his private land.

A cosy household
Fulk's house has a timber frame and walls made from a mixture of earth, clay and straw. The roof is thatched and there are wooden floorboards. The windows have no glass so they use wooden shutters at night.

Pork and porridge
The peasants wear linen or woollen clothes made from local material. They eat bread, porridge and home-grown vegetables, but have pork and bacon on special occasions. Their cow provides the milk.

The animals next door
Most houses have one room for the family and another for the animals. Agnes and Fulk also have a separate parlour. They fill any available space with food, which has to last them until the next harvest.

Little freedom
Villeins are tied to the land and can only leave if their overlord gives them permission. They must work on his land, use his mill and pay him *dues*, or fees, if they want to marry. As a result they are poor.

Kitchen

Bedroom

A growing village
The village is the centre of the manor and answers most of the people's needs, but its wealth depends on the produce from the land. In most manors the custom is to divide the arable land, land used for crops, into three large fields, and then give strips of land from these fields to the peasants.

Close to home
The villagers need little help from the outside world. They have a windmill to grind their grain, blacksmiths to shoe their horses and to make tools, and a bakery.

The village church
Everyone must give part of his crop to the church. The people like the village priest, who allows them to dance in the church yard, against the wishes of the bishop who is miles away.

Windmill

New houses

Baker

Blacksmith

The peasants' rights
The peasants are allowed to take hay from the meadow, graze their animals on common land and gather firewood in the forest, where their pigs can eat acorns.

The fun of the fair
The village fair is the great excitement twice a year. Traders buy the excellent wool produced from the manor, and sell things that are not usually available in the village.

Song and dance
Some wandering players have arrived to entertain. A *jester*, or clown, dances with his dog, while another plays music to his dancing bear. A puppet theatre attracts a small crowd.

The manor house
The lord of the manor's house is the largest of all the houses in the area, and usually built of stone. The steep roof has slates and the windows are glazed with small panes of glass.

Stables

Inn

BROTHER WILLIAM'S MONASTERY

You have followed the dusty track leading over the river and out of the village, and find yourself looking down at the buildings of the monastery.

During the Middle Ages, many people devoted their lives to God by becoming monks and nuns. These people made serious vows in which they promised to serve God and give up the comforts and luxuries of normal life. Prayer took up a major part of their day, but they also had to farm to provide food for the monastery or nunnery, and look after the poor and sick from local villages.

In a monastery, the abbot was the head of the monks, or brothers. He led the services in the abbey and organized the many people working for the monastery, not all of whom were monks.

A different world
On these pages you can see that life in a medieval monastery is far from quiet. The lord of the manor's younger brother William is a monk, and as the new father prior, he assists the abbot.

Early to rise, early to bed
The monks sleep on hard wooden beds in a *dormitory*, a large room with lots of beds. To make time for the many services during the day, the brothers rise early in the morning and go to bed at sunset.

Fertile monastery gardens
The monks breed animals for meat and grow crops in some of the fields. There is an orchard and a walled vegetable garden. The monks grow many herbs for the kitchen and as medicines.

Silent prayer and noisy meetings
The *cloister* is a quiet square surrounded by *colonnades*, covered walks supported by pillars, where the monks can go during times of private prayer. Monks copy books by hand in the library, and discuss the day-to-day business in the *chapterhouse*.

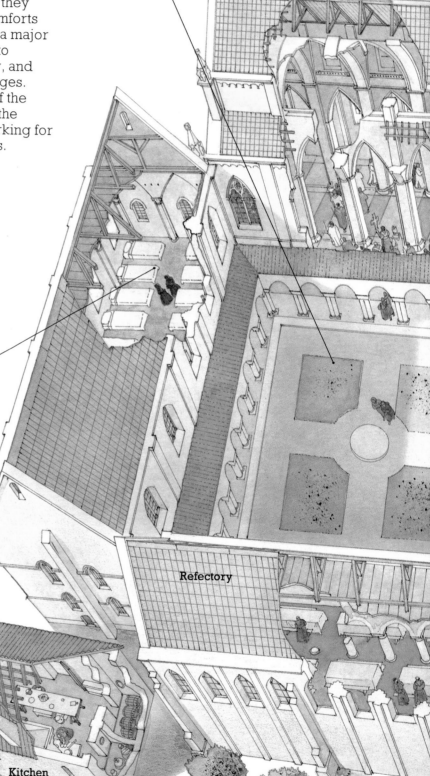

Refectory

Kitchen

The abbey
There are three services during the day and then *vespers* and *compline* at sunset and bedtime. People travel for miles to see the abbey's most precious *relic*, or holy remains – a piece of Christ's cross.

The wealth of the church
The monastery is wealthy. Brother William rents out any fields they are not using for a fee. Some noblemen and merchants, rich traders, also give money to the monastery.

Eating habits
The monks eat together in the *refectory* while one of them reads aloud from a religious book. Brother Dennis, as the *almoner*, arranges food and clothing for the poor.

Comforting strangers
The abbot has his own house where important visitors stay. The monks also have a duty to offer hospitality to travellers, so Brother Paul, as the *hospitaller*, arranges this.

Caring for the sick
The *infirmary* is where the monks look after their sick or aged brother monks. It is Brother Peter's job as the *infirmarer* to arrange nursing for the sick men who visit the monastery.

The school
There is a school to teach the child *novices*, young boys training to become monks, and boys who are sent by their parents for an education because there are no other schools.

57

THE ITALIAN RENAISSANCE

You have headed south across the English Channel, through France, and into northern Italy. It is A.D. 1450 and you are in the town of San Vitale during a time called the Renaissance.

The Renaissance, which means "rebirth", started in Italy but spread to most of Europe. It lasted from about A.D. 1450–1650. During this period a new way of thinking blossomed; people living in medieval Europe had not questioned the world around them, during the Renaissance they wanted to understand everything: the universe, nature, and how their bodies worked. They were fascinated by ancient Greece and Rome, and studied the art, architecture and philosophy of those times.

Northern Italian cities were wealthy from trade. There were rich *patrons*, men who supported artists, who encouraged great Renaissance men, such as Leonardo da Vinci and Michelangelo, to create marvellous works of art.

A successful man in San Vitale
Here you can see into the world of the wealthy Renaissance banker Francesco Gattadoro and his family. He is an important man in the town and the tradesmen treat him with great respect.

Cloth merchant

Working together
The *guilds*, groups of skilled workers who came together in the Middle Ages to protect their crafts, still exist in San Vitale. Each trade has its own area in the town.

A touch of spice
Producing wool and making cloth and leather goods are San Vitale's important trades. Some merchants do business with Eastern traders and sell rare spices.

Furs and finery
The wealthy citizens wear embroidered clothes decorated with furs and fine jewellery, accompanied by elaborate headresses. The poorer people dress in plain woollen cloth.

A true picture
Francesco drops in to see his new portrait. The artist has painted his patron with great realism and Francesco likes the way he appears in it, holding a small Roman statue.

The printed word
This craftsman has come from Germany with a new invention – a printing press. He can print a book in a few days. Before it took months to copy a book by hand.

Local bargains
The shops open out on to the streets through arches, rather as in ancient Rome. San Vitale's cloth shop is large and well stocked because northern Italy is famous for its fine wool.

Value for money
The Christian church disapproves of charging fees for loans. But Francesco's bank, which lends money, is now an essential part of the town and has many customers.

Plasterers and painters
Skilled men are working on a new brick building. They have used thin layers of marble to decorate the outside of the top storey, and they are plastering a lower wall for a fresco.

59

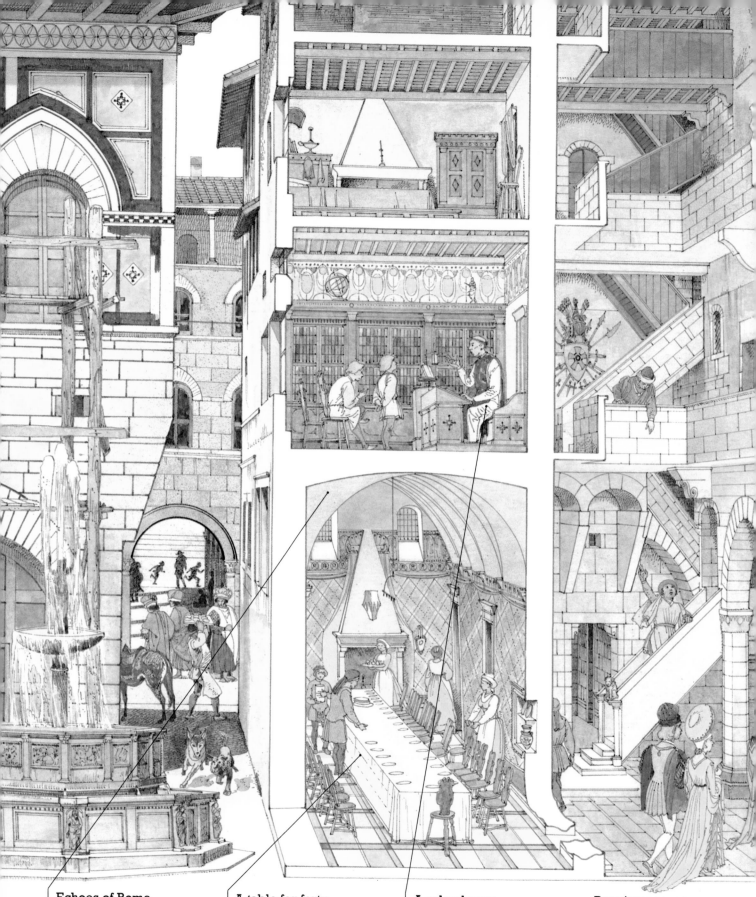

Echoes of Rome
Francesco's house shows his love of ancient Roman architecture. There are arches and pillars, and the banqueting room has a *barrel vaulted* ceiling, in which arches form a tunnel.

A table for forty
Servants set the table with fine glass jugs and goblets made locally, silver-ware and painted dishes. Forks are new additions – before people used knives, spoons and their fingers.

A schoolroom
Francesco makes sure that his son Giovanni is highly educated. He employs a priest to teach science, mathematics, history and Greek and Latin. Katrina is also an excellent scholar.

Renaissance manners
Besides his normal studies, Giovanni writes poems, sings, plays the lute, hunts, fights and is polite to everyone. Such skills and manners are admired and respected in these times.

A question of power

Here you can see inside Francesco's grand house, called a palazzo, *which looks on to a fountain in one of the main squares in San Vitale. The house is full of people because Francesco is celebrating the betrothal of his daughter Katrina, by giving a lavish banquet. He has chosen a rich husband for her who is connected to the great Medici family, who rule the nearby city of Florence.*

Like most rich Renaissance men Francesco knows that his position of power depends on the success of his business, and on having powerful friends. A closer link to the plans and actions of the powerful Medici family will help.

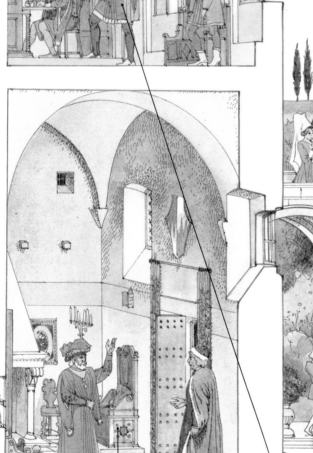

Living in style
Francesco's house is luxurious; the rooms are decorated with frescoes and wall hangings. Over the fireplace are stone overmantles and upstairs the ceilings are wooden.

Sitting comfortably
The wooden furniture is made with decorative panels, or painted. A throne-like chair is in the office, and upstairs the tutor sits at a desk with a bookshelf and lantern.

A patient crowd
Francesco has an office where he can talk business in private. In the room above, a poet is preparing a poem to entertain the guests, who by now have assembled in the garden.

In the shade
Behind the palazzo is a large garden that has been carefully designed to display Francesco's marble statues. A covered walkway and newly planted trees provide welcome shade.

CLUES TO THE PAST

About 150 years ago archaeology was treated like a treasure hunt, and some of the people looking for treasure were little better than robbers. Other people collected less valuable items such as flint spear heads, simply because they found them interesting. But there were also people who realized that if they carefully excavated a *site*, an area of land where people settled centuries ago, they could discover a lot about the lives of those settlers.

Today archaeologists are more like detectives, using the latest scientific equipment to help unravel the clues to the past. When excavating or "on a dig", they remove the soil with brushes and trowels, to avoid damaging remains or missing clues. They record every detail about a site and study everything they find, however broken or small, so they gradually build up a picture of how people lived. Whether they find a coin, a ship, or a horse's headdress, it is a vital clue.

Buried treasure
Remains from other times can be preserved for hundreds or thousands of years, depending on luck or on the conditions in which they are buried. Here you can see what can be discovered.

Stepping-stones to history
Some ancient buildings are still standing, but most have been reduced to ruins or buried underground. An archaeologist needs skill and training to know how to reconstruct a ruined building, and to find out how and why it was built.

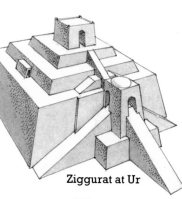

Ziggurat at Ur

Celtic weapons

Secrets from the dead
Unless they are purposely mummified, human bodies decay when they are buried in the ground. But some special conditions – hot sand, a bog, or ice – will preserve them so that we can tell what the people looked like, what they wore and why they died.

Peat bog man

Games for eternity
Toys often give clues about the world in which children once lived. Archaeologists in Egypt have also found models showing activities, such as preparing food, that were buried with the dead person to help him or her in the afterlife.

War and peace
Finding many weapons on a site or in tombs usually means that the people were either war-like by nature, or constantly under threat of attack. Tools show how the people worked the land and how skilled the craftsmen were.

Egyptian wall painting

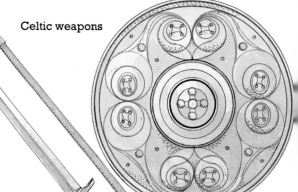

Egyptian toy boat

A colourful past
The tomb paintings found in Egypt and sometimes elsewhere, give us a picture of the daily lives and religious beliefs of the people buried there.

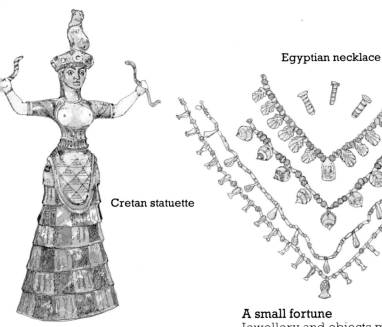
Cretan statuette

Egyptian necklace

Greek pot

Figure it out
Statues of kings and noblemen give us clues about their appearances, clothes, artistic tastes and even characters. We can tell how people imagined their gods from statues, and shrines reveal how they worshipped.

A small fortune
Jewellery and objects made of precious stones and metals tell us about the wealth of their owners and the skill of their makers. We try to find out where they were made and if the gems were imported. If so, how were they paid for, or were they stolen?

Historical pots
Pottery provides useful clues. It had little value, so tomb-robbers ignored it and modern equipment can date it accurately. Since pots were not handed down from one generation to the next, objects found with them can also be dated.

Script on a tablet from Ur

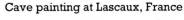
Cave painting at Lascaux, France

Read between the lines
The written word is the most valuable source of information, but some scripts are very hard to decipher. When they can be read, archaeologists must remember that rulers often ''bent'' the truth.

Magic paintings
Cave paintings are superb decorations, but people now think they were done for a purpose. Did the painters believe they could magically increase the numbers of animals, or did the paintings bring the hunters good luck?

Dark secrets
Most people from the past believed in a life after death, and hoped to take their possessions with them by placing them in the tombs. As a result, tombs give archaeologists a lot of information, as long as the robbers have not got there first.

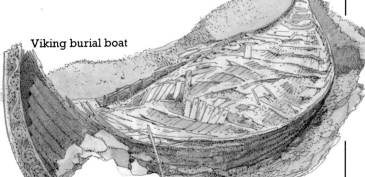
Viking burial boat

Roman coins

Heads or tails?
Coins are useful as they allow a date to be given to the site in which they are found. Coins found far away from where they were made are a puzzle. Were they paid to foreign soldiers, used in trade, or were they raiders' loot?

INDEX